COOL JOBS

for Handy Helpers

Ways to Make Money Doing Home Services

Pam Scheunemann

ABDO
Publishing Company

Visit us at www.abdopublishing.com

Published by ABDO Publishing Company, 8000 West 78th Street, Edina, Minnesota 55439.

Printed in the United States , North Mankato, Minnesota
052010
092010

 PRINTED ON RECYCLED PAPER

Design and Production: Kelly Doudna, Mighty Media, Inc.
Series Editor: Liz Salzmann
Photo Credits: Kelly Doudna, iStockPhoto (buchwerkstatt.
com, Nina Shannon, Rick Sargeant), Shutterstock
Money Savvy Pig® photo courtesy of Money Savvy
Generation/www.msgen.com

**Library of Congress
Cataloging-in-Publication Data**

Scheunemann, Pam, 1955-
   Cool jobs for handy helpers : ways to make money doing
home services / Pam Scheunemann.
       p. cm. -- (Cool kid jobs)
   Includes index.
   ISBN 978-1-61613-195-1
   1. Money-making projects for children--Juvenile literature. 2.
Helping behavior--Juvenile literature. 3. Success in business
--Juvenile literature. 4. Finance, Personal--Juvenile literature.
I. Title.
   HF5392.S333 2011
   640.23--dc22
                            2010004311

NOTE TO ADULTS

A job can be a good learning experience for you and your child. Be sure to encourage your child to discuss his or her job ideas with you. Talk about the risks and the benefits. Set up some rules for your child's safety with regard to:

* working with strangers

* transportation to and from the job

* proper and safe use of tools or equipment

* giving out phone numbers or e-mail addresses

* emergency contacts

Contents

Why Work?

There are a lot of reasons to have a job. The first one you probably think of is to earn money. But you can get more out of a job than just money. You can learn new skills, meet new people, and get some experience.

MAKING MONEY

When you do a job such as washing cars or windows, you are providing a service. If people pay you for your service, you can earn some money!

BESIDES MONEY

You will gain more than money from having a job. You also get work experience and learn about being responsible. That means showing up on time, keeping your word, and being trustworthy.

Volunteering is doing a job you don't get paid for. But you can earn other rewards. You can learn new skills that will help you get other jobs. And you can feel good about helping out!

What Can You Do with Your Money?

There are four things you can do with the money you earn.

SAVE

Saving is keeping your money in a safe place. You add money a little at a time as you earn it. Soon you could save enough for something such as a new bike.

SPEND

Spending is using your money to buy things you want. Maybe you want to go to a movie or buy a new computer game.

DONATE

It is important to give some of your earnings to organizations that help others.

INVEST

Investing is saving for long-term goals such as college expenses.

Ask your parents to help you decide how much money to use for each purpose. You'll be glad you did!

Money Savvy Pig®

What's Your Plan?

Each state has laws about kids working. If you are too young to work at a regular job, you can create your own job. Whatever job you try, you should have a plan.

WHAT WILL YOU DO?

Your job should relate to your abilities and likes. Make a list of the kinds of helpful things you know how to do. Which do you like doing the most? That's a good place to start!

WHO ARE YOUR CUSTOMERS?

Who needs your product or service? Where will you find your customers? How will you let people know about your services?

WHERE WILL YOU DO THE WORK?

Will you work at your house, the customers' homes, or another location?

SETTING REALISTIC GOALS

A goal is something you are working toward. When you set your job goals, keep these things in mind:

* Do you have permission from your parents?

* Is your idea something you already know how to do?

* Will this job interfere with your schoolwork or other activities?

* Are there any costs to start your job? Do you have the money or do you need to get a loan?

* Are there tools or **materials** you need to start your job? Will you continue to need supplies?

* Will you work alone or with a friend? How will you divide the work and the money you make?

What If It Doesn't Work?

Don't get **discouraged** if things don't work out the way you planned. Think about what you could have done differently and try again!

Get Permission

You must get permission from a parent or **guardian** before you work for someone else. Give your parents all of the details about the job.

WHO WILL YOU BE WORKING FOR?

Are you working for a relative or friend of the family? If not, your parents should meet your customer.

WHEN WILL YOU BE WORKING?

What day will you start the work? What time? Will your services be needed once or more often?

WHERE IS THE JOB?

Be sure your family has the address and phone number of where you are working. Create a Customer Information form similar to the one on page 15. Fill out a form for each customer.

HOW WILL YOU GET THERE?

Is your job within walking or biking distance? Do you need a ride there? Is it okay for you to take the bus to get there? What if it's during the evening or after dark?

WHO ELSE WILL BE THERE?

Are you going to do the job alone or with a friend? Will there be other people around while you are working?

WHAT IS EXPECTED OF YOU?

Are you clear about the job you were hired to do? Have you made an agreement with the customer about what is expected of you (see page 14)?

Be Smart, Be Safe

Talk with your parents about working for strangers. Always tell your parents where you are going and what time they should expect you to be home. Make sure they have a phone number where they can reach you while you are working.

HANDY HELPER SAFETY

It is important to be sure you know how to use the tools for helping around the house. Be careful when using sharp tools. Stretch a bit before you start doing a lot of **physical** work. Learn the proper way to lift heavy objects.

Be careful with all cleaning products. Don't ever mix bleach with a product that has ammonia in it. The combination of these chemicals creates fumes that can make you sick.

Getting the Word Out

Okay, you've decided what to do. Now how do you get the work? There are different ways to get the word out.

BUSINESS CARDS

A simple business card can be very helpful in getting customers. Give cards to the people you talk to about your business. Maybe even give each person an extra so he or she can pass one along to a friend.

Your business card should have your name, your business name, and your phone number. Get permission from a parent before putting your home address, phone number, or e-mail address on a card.

WORD OF MOUTH

Let as many people know about your business as you can. They'll tell other people, and those people will tell more people, and so on.

Make Your Own Business Cards

1 On a piece of white paper, draw a rectangle with a black pen. It should be 3½ x 2 inches (9 x 5 cm). Design your business card inside the rectangle.

2 Make 11 copies of the card. Cut each one out, including the original. Cut outside the border so the lines show.

3 Glue the cards onto a piece of 8½ x 11-inch (22 x 28 cm) paper. Leave a ¼-inch (½ cm) border around the edge of the paper. This is your business card **master**.

4 Copy the master onto card stock. If you're using a black-and-white copier, try using colored card stock. Or, use white card stock and add color with markers or colored pencils.

5 Cut out your business cards. When you run out of cards, make more copies of your master.

WHAT YOU'LL NEED

white paper
ruler
black pen
copier
scissors

glue
card stock (white or colored)
markers or colored pencils

Extra Hands Home Services

James and Rick Hunter
1911 Address Drive
Kansas City, KS
(913) 555-0152

PRO TIP
Use the computer to make your flyer and cards. Or, follow the steps here and on page 13 for a more personal touch.

11

Extra Hands Home Services

Do you need reliable help around your home?

- ❀ Trash Removal
- ❀ Gift Wrapping
- ❀ Coupon Clipping
- ❀ Car Washing
- ❀ Cleaning
- ❀ Window Washing

Extra Hands Home Services can help!

- ❀ Experienced in lawn care
- ❀ Reasonable rates

Call James or Rick Hunter for an estimate (913) 555-0152

Extra Hands Home Services (913) 555-0152 | Extra Hands Home Services (913) 555-0152 | Extra Hands Home Services (913) 555-0152 | Extra Hands Home Services (913) 555-0152 | Extra Hands Home Services (913) 555-0152 | Extra Hands Home Services (913) 555-0152 | Extra Hands Home Services (913) 555-0152 | Extra Hands Home Services (913) 555-0152 | Extra Hands Home Services (913) 555-0152 | Extra Hands Home Services (913) 555-0152 | Extra Hands Home Services (913) 555-0152 | Extra Hands Home Services (913) 555-0152 | Extra Hands Home Services (913) 555-0152 | Extra Hands Home Services (913) 555-0152 | Extra Hands Home Services (913) 555-0152 | Extra Hands Home Services (913) 555-0152 | Extra Hands Home Services (913) 555-0152 | Extra Hands Home Services (913) 555-0152

A flyer is a one-page sheet about your product or service. You can include more information than will fit on a business card. Make little mini cards at the bottom of the flyer for people to tear off. Include your service and phone number. Get your parent's permission first! Give flyers to people you know. Also, some places have bulletin boards for flyers:

- ✳ apartment building lobbies
- ✳ stores
- ✳ community centers
- ✳ schools
- ✳ places of worship

Make Your Own Flyer

1 Design a **master** copy of your flyer on a sheet of white paper that is 8½ x 11 inches (22 x 28 cm).

2 Use bright colors so your flyer will stand out. If you plan to use a black-and-white copier, use black on the master and copy it onto colored paper.

3 Remember that copiers won't copy anything written too close to the edge of the master. So leave a border of at least ¼ inch (½ cm) on all sides.

4 Make as many copies of the master as you need. Cut the lines between the mini cards so customers can tear them off easily.

WHAT YOU'LL NEED

white paper

black pen

ruler

markers or colored pencils

copier

colored paper (optional)

scissors

Money Matters

One reason to work is so you can make money!

Here are some hints about money.

Sample form: make yours fit your business!

Extra Hands Customer Agreement

Customer Name _____
Address _____
_____
Phone _____
Job Description _____
_____
_____

Schedule

MONDAY	TUESDAY	WEDNESDAY	THURSDAY	FRIDAY	SATURDAY	SUNDAY

Rate/Payment Agreement

Customer agrees to pay Extra Hands Home Services
$_____ for the services listed above in the job
description for each [hour, day, week, month].

Payments will be made on a [per visit, weekly, monthly] basis.

_____
Customer Signature   Date

Extra Hands Home Services
James and Rick Hunter
1911 Address Drive, Kansas City, KS
(913) 555-0152

HOW MUCH SHOULD YOU CHARGE?

Here are things to consider when figuring out what to charge.

* Find out what other people charge for the same product or service.

* Are you providing tools or supplies? Make sure you charge enough to cover your costs.

* Do you want to charge by the hour or by the job? Will you charge less if they are steady customers?

Make an Agreement

Be clear with your customer about how much you are charging. Discuss the details with the customer.

🍂 Extra Hands Customer Information

Customer:	
Address:	
Phone Number:	
Emergency Phone Numbers:	
Owner:	
Neighbor:	
House Information (keys, locks, security system, flashlights, fire extinguisher, etc.)	
Tools/Supplies Information (location and type of cleaning supplies and equipment)	
Tools/Supplies to Bring from Home (cleaning supplies and equipment)	
Instructions	

Extra Hands Home Services
James and Rick Hunter
1911 Address Drive, Kansas City, KS
(913) 555-0152

Sample form: make yours fit your business!

Then write them down on a Customer Agreement form. You and the customer should each have a copy of the Agreement.

KNOW YOUR CUSTOMERS

Fill out a Customer Information form for each customer. Keep them in a folder with the Customer Agreements. Update the forms if anything changes.

HOW MUCH DID YOU MAKE?

Profit is the amount of money you have left after you subtract your expenses. If you are only charging for your time, it's all profit, right? Not so fast! Did you have to make flyers or business cards? Did you provide supplies to do the job?

Add up your expenses. Subtract the expenses from the amount you earned. The amount left over is your profit.

15

Car Washing Wonder

Washing a car can take a lot of time, which not everyone has. That's why they need you!

WHAT YOU'LL NEED

plastic bucket

hose/water supply

car washing soap

car washing sponge or cloth

soft cotton towels

window cleaner

vacuum cleaner

trash bags

step stool

BEFORE YOU BEGIN

Determine where you will wash the car. You could do it at the customer's home. Or the customer could bring the car to your home.

Make sure you have permission to use the water supply and any hoses or other equipment.

Round up all the supplies you need. Keep track of how much you spend on supplies. Make sure that you include part of that cost in your price.

Find out if there are any special instructions. Some people are picky about how their cars get washed. Fill out a Customer Agreement form (see page 14). Write down all the details for the job.

Make a big sign to put in your yard that advertises your car wash services. Put it out while you are washing a car.

ON THE JOB

* Do some research on the proper way to wash a car. There are special soaps, cleaners, sponges, and cloths for use on cars.

* Don't forget to clean the wheels and hubcaps. There are special cleaners for those too!

* Be sure to wash the insides and outsides of the windows.

* The customer may want you to clean the inside. Take everything out of the car. Have a safe, dry place to put it. Vacuum thoroughly.

* Make sure you put everything back when you are done.

PRO TIP
Learn how to wax a car. You can charge more for extra services!

Coupon Clipper

Using **coupons** is a good way to save money. But people often just don't have the time. Finding, clipping, and organizing coupons isn't as easy as it seems.

WHAT YOU'LL NEED
current newspapers and magazines
weekly store ads
scissors
pen
storage container
index cards or dividers (optional)

BEFORE YOU BEGIN

Meet with the customer to get a list of products the customer buys. Agree on when and how often you will give the **coupons** to the customer. Fill out a Customer Agreement form (see page 14). Write down all the details for the job.

Have a container ready to store the coupons in. Shoeboxes, envelopes, zipper bags, and file boxes work well. If you use a box, buy dividers, or make them out of index cards.

Make a Coupon Box

Find a box that you can decorate for your customer. Make dividers for the different coupon categories. That will make it easy to find the right coupon!

DO GOOD
People in the military are allowed to use expired coupons. Find a military family to give your expired coupons to.

ON THE JOB

* Look through current newspapers and magazines. Cut out coupons for the things on your customer's list.

* Organize the coupons by type of product. Put them in alphabetical order. For example: bread, cereal, cleaning supplies, frozen food, meat, pet supplies.

* Circle the **expiration** date on each coupon. That makes it easier to quickly see if the coupon has expired.

* Clip coupons at the same time each week. It's helpful to have a routine. At the beginning of each clipping session, remove any coupons that have expired.

* Also clip coupons for products that are similar to the ones on your customer's list. The customer may want to try something new.

Crystal Clear Window Washing

Washing windows is many people's least favorite job. It probably won't be hard to find people who will hire you to do it!

BEFORE YOU BEGIN

The windows in each house will be a little different. Some windows can be tilted so you can wash the inside and outside. Have the customer show you how the windows should be cleaned.

Fill out a Customer Agreement form (see page 14). Write down all the details for the job.

Try washing windows at home to get some practice.

ON THE JOB

✳ First wipe down the frame and the windowsill. Use the sponge and bucket of water.

✳ Then spray the glass with window cleaner. Wipe with a rag. Make sure you clean all the way to the edges. Change rags when they get too wet or dirty.

✳ Use a stepladder to reach higher windows. Never use a regular ladder by yourself. And never stand on the top step of a stepladder! If a window is too high for you to reach, don't clean it. Safety always comes first.

✳ You can also offer to clean the screens. Take the screens outside and use a hose to clean them.

GO GREEN!
Save money and the environment! Make your own window cleaner. Mix equal amounts of vinegar and water.

Grand Gift Wrapping

People wrap gifts for many occasions. Around the holidays people are most likely to need help.

WHAT YOU'LL NEED

wrapping paper or fabric
gift bags
ribbon and bows
scissors
tape
package decorations
gift tags
paper and pencil
empty boxes

BEFORE YOU BEGIN

Decide if you will wrap the gifts at your house or your customer's house. Have the customer list the gifts and who each one is for.

Ask if there are any special instructions. Maybe the customer wants you to use certain colors or types of bows.

Fill out a Customer Agreement form (see page 14). Write down all the details for the job.

Save different-sized boxes to use for wrapping gifts. Have a **variety** of wrapping **materials** available. Be creative!

Set up a table to work on. Take one along if you work at someone else's house.

ON THE JOB

✳ Wrap some small, empty boxes to show as examples. You can label or number them. That makes it easier for your customers to say how they want their gifts wrapped.

✳ Look at magazines, online, or in craft shops to get new gift-wrapping ideas.

✳ Offer package decorations. You can charge extra for them.

✳ Wrapping paper and ribbon is often on sale after the holidays. Stock up for use during the year.

✳ Find out if you can set up a gift-wrapping service at a mall, store, or community center.

GO GREEN
Think about what recycled materials can be used to wrap gifts.

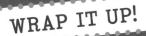

There are many **materials** you can use for wrapping gifts. The sky is the limit! Try some of these ideas and don't be afraid to experiment!

Send an old map on a new journey as gift wrap. Add a brightly colored ribbon for a fresh look.

PAPER

Lunch bags aren't just for lunch anymore. They come in many sizes and colors.

Kraft paper comes in large rolls. It can be painted, stamped, or decorated with stickers or paper doilies.

Learn about furoshiki, a traditional Japanese style of wrapping with cloth. The fabric can be reused many times, or made into something else!

FABRIC

Purchase tulle bags in different colors. Line the bags with scraps of fabric to cover the gift.

DECORATIONS AND GIFT TAGS

* Find decorations in nature. Try using leaves, twigs, or pinecones to adorn gifts. Don't use berries. They will rot, and they can be **dangerous** to children and pets.

* Look for old trinkets around the house that would be cute on a package or a tag.

* Try decorating some round paper key tags.

* Fold a small piece of colored paper to make a gift tag. Decorate it with stickers, glitter paint, or markers.

Be a Cleaning Machine

There are lots of different types of cleaning to do around the house. Cleaning can range from dusting a chair to organizing a closet. Just let people know you're available!

WHAT YOU'LL NEED

bucket and mop
vacuum cleaner
clean rags or cloths
trash bags
stepladder
cleaning products

SAFETY TIP
Don't mix different cleaning products together. For example, mixing bleach and ammonia creates **dangerous** fumes.

BEFORE YOU BEGIN

Each person has his or her own way of cleaning. Have the customer show you exactly what you are expected to do.

Your customer may want you to use special cleaning products. Discuss with your customer who will supply the equipment and cleaning supplies.

Fill out a Customer Agreement form (see page 14). Write down all the details for the job.

ON THE JOB

Generally, you should clean each room from top to bottom. Check for cobwebs in the corners of the ceiling first. Then wipe down light fixtures and ceiling fans. Only do this if you can reach them safely. Window blinds and sills should be next, and then the furniture. Clean the floor last. The next few sections offer room-by-room tips.

THE BATHROOM

* Clean the tub and shower. Wipe the walls and scrub the tub or shower floor.

* Clean the mirror. Scrub the sink and faucets.

* Clean the countertop and anything sitting on the countertop.

* Wipe off shelves and any items on the shelves.

* Clean the inside of the toilet and flush it. Wipe the seat, lid, and outside of the toilet.

* Empty the trash.

* Shake out rugs. Sweep or vacuum and then wash the floor.

THE KITCHEN

Wipe the outsides of the cabinets.

Wash the countertop. Organize or clean any items sitting on the countertop.

Clean the **appliances**:

* microwave (inside and out)

* refrigerator (outside and top, see inside cleaning tips to the right)

* dishwasher (front)

* stove top and oven door

Wipe the table and chairs.

Scrub out the sink and clean the faucet.

Empty the trash and recycling.

Sweep or vacuum and then wash the floor.

CLEANING THE INSIDE OF THE REFRIGERATOR

Put all the food in a cooler with some ice until you are done cleaning. Throw away anything that is **expired** or spoiled.

Remove all drawers, racks, and shelves. Wash them in hot soapy water and rinse and dry them.

Wipe the refrigerator walls with a sprinkle of baking soda mixed in hot water. Rinse and dry the walls.

Wash the rubber around the edge of the door. Be sure to get into the cracks. Dry it thoroughly.

Replace all the drawers, racks, and shelves.

Put the food back in the refrigerator. Wipe off bottles and jars before putting them back.

THE BEDROOM

Clean any mirrors in the room.

Dust all the furniture. Don't forget the front, sides, and any shelves.

If it is a baby's room, clean the crib and changing table. Use a safe **disinfectant**.

Ask if your customer wants the sheets changed or put in the laundry. Make the bed if needed.

Wipe the baseboards.

Vacuum rugs or carpet. Use a dust mop on wood floors. Don't forget to clean under the bed!

SAVINGS TIP
Save half of the money you make. Think about what you'll buy with your earnings.

THE LIVING ROOM, DINING ROOM, AND HALLWAYS

Clean mirrors and glass doors on cabinets.

Dust all the furniture. Don't forget the front, sides, and any shelves.

Dust lamps and lamp shades.

Carefully dust or wipe **knickknacks**.

Clean electronics like the television and DVD player.

Wipe the baseboards.

Vacuum rugs or carpet. Use a dust mop on wood floors. Don't forget to clean under the furniture whenever possible.

Tips for Success

Success isn't measured just by how much money you make. How you look and behave is also important.

BE ON TIME

Show that you are responsible and follow through on your agreements.

BE POLITE

This means that you need to respect your customer. Do not interrupt. Ask any questions politely. Be respectful even if you don't agree with someone.

DRESS FOR THE JOB

Be neat and clean, even if it's a dirty job! Wear the right clothing for the job.

BE ON THE SAFE SIDE

Follow safety instructions. Review tool or equipment safety before you start a job. Never try to use a tool or machine that you are not familiar with. Always have **emergency** contact information.

ALWAYS COMPLETE THE JOB

Remember the agreement you made? You need to follow through and do everything you agreed to do. Put away all tools and supplies you use. If you are messy or don't finish a job, you probably won't be hired again!

THIS IS JUST THE BEGINNING

Okay, it is the end of the book. But, it is just the beginning for you! This book has provided information about some ways to make money. Now decide what might work for you. Talk it over with your parents. And don't forget to have some fun!

Glossary

appliance – a machine that does a special job.

coupon – a piece of paper that offers a discount on a service or product.

dangerous – able or likely to cause harm or injury.

discouraged – feeling that you can't do something, or that something isn't worth trying.

disinfectant – a chemical used to kill germs.

emergency – a sudden, unexpected, dangerous situation that requires immediate attention.

expire – to be unusable because too much time has passed. An *expiration date* is the day something will become unusable.

guardian – the person who, by law, cares for a minor.

knickknack – a small object put on a shelf or table for decoration.

master – an original copy that is reproduced to make more of the same thing.

material – the substance something is made of, such as metal, fabric, or plastic.

physical – having to do with the body.

variety – a collection of different types of one thing. An assortment.

volunteer – to offer to do a job, most often without pay.

WEB SITES

To learn more about the jobs that kids can do, visit ABDO Publishing Company on the World Wide Web at www.abdopublishing.com. Web sites about creative ways for kids to earn money are featured on our Book Links page. These links are routinely monitored and updated to provide the most current information available.

Index